Math in F⊙cus®

Singapore Math®
by Marshall Cavendish

Extra Practice
and Homework

Program Consultant
Dr. Fong Ho Kheong

Marshall Cavendish
Education

U.S. Distributor

Houghton Mifflin Harcourt.
The Learning Company™

Course
3A

© 2020 Marshall Cavendish Education Pte Ltd

Published by Marshall Cavendish Education
Times Centre, 1 New Industrial Road, Singapore 536196
Customer Service Hotline: (65) 6213 9688
US Office Tel: (1-914) 332 8888 | Fax: (1-914) 332 8882
E-mail: cs@mceducation.com
Website: www.mceducation.com

Distributed by
Houghton Mifflin Harcourt
125 High Street
Boston, MA 02110
Tel: 617-351-5000
Website: www.hmhco.com/programs/math-in-focus

First published 2020

ISBN 978-0-358-10312-7

Printed in Singapore

2 3 4 5 6 7 8 9   1401   25 24 23 22
4500840184   B C D E

The cover image shows a rockhopper penguin.
Rockhopper penguins live in the cold waters of South America, South Africa, and Antarctica. They feed on small fish, krill, or squid. A unique characteristic is the yellow crest on their heads. They are amazing swimmers, but are also very agile on land, getting their name from the way they leap effortlessly over rocks. There are no distinct differences in physical characteristics between the males and females so a DNA test is required to check the gender of a rockhopper penguin.

Contents

Chapter 1   **The Real Number System**

Activity 1	Introducing Irrational Numbers	1
Activity 2	Introducing the Real Number System	3
Activity 3	Introducing Significant Digits	5
Math Journal		9
Put On Your Thinking Cap!		10

Chapter 2   **Exponents**

Activity 1	Exponential Notation	11
Activity 2	The Product and the Quotient of Powers	13
Activity 3	The Power of a Power	15
Activity 4	The Power of a Product and the Power of a Quotient	17
Activity 5	Zero and Negative Exponents	19
Activity 6	Squares, Square Roots, Cubes and Cube Roots	23
Math Journal		25
Put On Your Thinking Cap!		26

Chapter 3   **Scientific Notation**

Activity 1	Understanding Scientific Notation	27
Activity 2	Adding and Subtracting in Scientific Notation	31
Activity 3	Multiplying and Dividing in Scientific Notation	35
Math Journal		39
Put On Your Thinking Cap!		40

Chapter 4   **Linear Equations and Inequalities**

Activity 1	Solving Linear Equations with One Variable	41
Activity 2	Identifying the Number of Solutions to a Linear Equation	45
Activity 3	Understanding Linear Equations with Two Variables	49
Activity 4	Solving for a Variable in a Two-Variable Linear Equation	55
Activity 5	Solving Linear Inequalities with One Variable	59
Math Journal		61
Put On Your Thinking Cap!		62

Chapter 5 **Lines and Linear Equations**

Activity 1   Finding and Interpreting Slopes of Lines   **63**

Activity 2   Understanding Slope-Intercept Form   **67**

Activity 3   Writing Linear Equations   **71**

Activity 4   Sketching Graphs of Linear Equations   **75**

Activity 5   Real-World Problems: Linear Equations   **81**

Math Journal   **87**

Put On Your Thinking Cap!   **88**

Chapter 6 **Systems of Linear Equations**

Activity 1   Introduction to Systems of Linear Equations   **89**

Activity 2   Solving Systems of Linear Equations Using Algebraic Methods   **93**

Activity 3   Real-World Problems: Systems of Linear Equations   **99**

Activity 4   Solving Systems of Linear Equations by Graphing   **107**

Activity 5   Inconsistent and Dependent Systems of Linear Equations   **113**

Math Journal   **117**

Put On Your Thinking Cap!   **118**

Preface

Welcome!

Math in Focus® *Extra Practice and Homework* is written to complement the Student Edition in your learning journey.

The book provides carefully constructed activities and problems that parallel what you have learned in the Student Edition.

- **Activities** are designed to help you achieve proficiency in the math concepts and to develop confidence in your mathematical abilities.

- **MATH JOURNAL** is included to provide you with opportunities to reflect on the learning in the chapter.

- **PUT ON YOUR THINKING CAP!** allows you to improve your critical thinking and problem-solving skills, as well as to be challenged as you solve problems in novel ways.

You may use a calculator whenever appears.

BLANK

Name: _____ Date: _____

Chapter 2
Extra Practice and Homework
Exponents

Activity 1   Exponential Notation

Determine whether each statement is correct. If it is incorrect, state the reason.

1 $17^4 = 17 \cdot 17 \cdot 17 \cdot 17$

2 $8^3 = (-8) \cdot (-8) \cdot (-8)$

Write each expression in exponential notation.

3 $27 \cdot 27 \cdot 27 \cdot 27$

4 $\dfrac{2}{9} \cdot \dfrac{2}{9} \cdot \dfrac{2}{9}$

5 $6.7 \cdot 6.7 \cdot 6.7 \cdot 6.7$

6 $(-9) \cdot (-9) \cdot (-9)$

Expand and evaluate each expression.

7 3^2

8 5^3

9 $\left(\dfrac{4}{9}\right)^3$

10 $(-8.8)^3$

Write the prime factorization of each number in exponential notation.

11 60

12 175

13 1,568

14 18,225

Solve.

15 Lilian folded a large piece of square paper along its diagonal. She noticed that two triangles were formed. Then, she made a second fold and four triangles were formed.

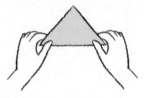  

The following table shows the result of her folds of the square paper.

Number of Folds	Number of Triangles Formed on Square Paper
1	2
2	4
3	8

How many folds must Lilian make to obtain 64 triangles on the square paper?

Extra Practice and Homework
Exponents

Activity 2   The Product and the Quotient of Powers

Simplify each expression. Write each answer in exponential notation.

1 $5^8 \cdot 5^2$

2 $3.2^4 \cdot 3.2^5$

3 $\left(\dfrac{7}{9}\right)^2 \cdot \left(\dfrac{7}{9}\right)^6$

4 $(-12)^8 \cdot (-12)$

5 $q^4 \cdot q^3$

6 $m^9 \div m^5$

7 $(-7)^9 \div (-7)^2$

8 $\left(\dfrac{3}{4}\right)^8 \div \left(\dfrac{3}{4}\right)^5$

9 $6xy^2 \cdot 3x^7y^2$

10 $4.5a^3b^7 \cdot 2a^6b$

11 $b^5c^8 \div b^3c^2$

12 $72x^9y^7 \div 8x^3y^5$

13 $\dfrac{8^9 \cdot 8^2 \cdot 8^6}{8^4 \cdot 8^2 \cdot 8^3}$

14 $\dfrac{\left(\frac{2}{3}\right)^7 \cdot \left(\frac{2}{3}\right)^3 \cdot \left(\frac{2}{3}\right)^9}{\left(\frac{2}{3}\right)^2 \cdot \left(\frac{2}{3}\right) \cdot \left(\frac{2}{3}\right)^4}$

15 $\dfrac{y^3 \cdot y^8 \cdot y^6}{y^4 \cdot y^2 \cdot y^2}$

16 $\dfrac{5a^5 \cdot 7b^4 \cdot 2b^4}{b^5 \cdot 5b^2 \cdot 2a^4}$

Chapter 2

Extra Practice and Homework
Exponents

Activity 3   The Power of a Power

Simplify each expression. Write each answer in exponential notation.

1 $(9^6)^4$

2 $(p^5)^4$

3 $\left[\left(\dfrac{6}{7}\right)^6\right]^3$

4 $[(4b)^4]^4$

5 $[(-22)^5]^7$

6 $[(-2q)^4]^2$

Remember to simplify the expression when the exponent of a negative number is even.

7 $(2^5 \cdot 2^3)^2$

8 $(q^7 \cdot q)^4$

9 $\left[\left(\dfrac{5}{6}\right)^3 \cdot \left(\dfrac{5}{6}\right)^2\right]^3$

10 $\left[\left(-\dfrac{9}{10}\right)^4 \cdot \left(-\dfrac{9}{10}\right)^8\right]^2$

11 $(11^6 \cdot 11^6)^2 \div 11^9$

12 $(y^9 \cdot y)^3 \div y^{13}$

13 $\dfrac{(3^3 \cdot 3^5)^4}{(3^8)^2}$

14 $\dfrac{(w^9 \cdot w^5)^4}{(w^2)^{11}}$

15 $(u^3 \cdot u^6)^4 \div 8u^2$

16 $(p^2 \cdot p^5)^9 \div 7p^3$

17 $\dfrac{\left(\frac{3}{7}\right)^5 \cdot \left(\frac{9}{7}\right)^2}{\left(\frac{3^4}{7^3}\right)^2}$

18 $\dfrac{\left(\frac{y}{5}\right)^2 \cdot \left(\frac{y^3}{5}\right)^5}{\left(\frac{y^2}{5}\right)^6}$

Extra Practice and Homework
Exponents

Activity 4 The Power of a Product and the Power of a Quotient

Simplify each expression. Write each answer in exponential notation.

1 $7^3 \cdot 4^3$

2 $8.3^5 \cdot 1.2^5$

3 $\left(\frac{3}{7}\right)^4 \cdot \left(\frac{1}{2}\right)^4$

4 $\left(-\frac{4}{5}\right)^6 \cdot \left(-\frac{2}{3}\right)^6$

5 $p^8 \cdot w^8$

6 $(6x)^3 \cdot (1.2y)^3$

7 $w^9 \div v^9$

8 $(8.2y)^4 \div (2x)^4$

9 $1.8^3 \div 0.3^3$

10 $12^9 \div 21^9$

11 $(-20)^2 \div (-5)^2$

12 $(p^6 \cdot q \cdot q^2)^3$

13 $\left(\dfrac{36b^3}{9a^5}\right)^3$

14 $\dfrac{8^7 \cdot 8^4 \cdot 2^3}{16^3}$

15 $\dfrac{(9^3)^4 \cdot 6^{12}}{27^{12}}$

16 $\dfrac{18^8}{6^3 \cdot 3^4 \cdot 6^5}$

Name: _____ Date: _____

Extra Practice and Homework
Exponents

Activity 5   Zero and Negative Exponents

Simplify each expression and evaluate.

1 $9^4 \cdot 9^0$

2 $11^3 \cdot (-11)^0$

3 $\left(\dfrac{6}{7}\right)^8 \cdot \left(\dfrac{6}{7}\right)^0$

4 $9^2 \cdot 10^3 + 5^3 \cdot 10^2 + 2^6 \cdot 10^0$

5 $4.7 \cdot 10^3 + 6 \cdot 10^2 + 7 \cdot 10^0$

6 $\dfrac{5^3 \cdot 5^7}{5^{10}}$

7 $(4^{-2})^0 \cdot 7^2$

8 $\dfrac{(8^{-4})^{-2} \cdot 7^8}{56^8}$

Simplify each expression. Write each answer using a negative exponent.

9 $6^{-8} \cdot 6^3$

10 $\dfrac{(-9)^{-4}}{(-9)^4}$

11 $\dfrac{5}{6} \div \left[\left(\dfrac{5}{6}\right)^7 \cdot \left(\dfrac{5}{6}\right)^0\right]$

12 $\left(\dfrac{3}{8}\right)^{-5} \cdot \left(\dfrac{3}{8}\right)^{-2} \div \left(\dfrac{3}{8}\right)^{-1}$

13 $\dfrac{y^0}{y^4 \cdot y^3}$

14 $\dfrac{7p^{-6} \cdot 6p^{-3}}{3p^{-5}}$

Simplify each expression. Write each answer using a positive exponent.

15 $4.1^0 \div 3.6^5$

16 $9.6^{-4} \div 3.2^{-4}$

17 $\dfrac{(-6)^{-8}}{(-6)^3}$

18 $\left(\dfrac{4}{9}\right)^{-7} \cdot \left(\dfrac{4}{9}\right)^{-1} \div \left(\dfrac{4}{9}\right)^{-5}$

19 $\dfrac{5h^{-2} \cdot 7h^{-4}}{25h^{-9}}$

20 $\dfrac{b^{16} \cdot b^{-5}}{b^{-7}}$

Simply each expression and evaluate where applicable.

21 $\dfrac{4^{-3} \cdot 4^0}{9^4 \cdot 9^{-7}}$

22 $\dfrac{(5^{-2})^4 \cdot 16^{-8}}{40^{-8}}$

23 $\dfrac{6^0}{3^{-3} \cdot 2^{-3}}$

24 $\dfrac{(5^3)^{-4}}{10^{-8} \cdot (-2)^5}$

25 $\left(\dfrac{8v^6}{-64w^0}\right)^{-1}$

26 $\dfrac{28x^4y^7}{4x^6y^{-1}}$

Chapter 2 Extra Practice and Homework
Exponents

Activity 6 Squares, Square Roots, Cubes, and Cube Roots

Find the two square roots of each number. Round each answer to the nearest tenth where applicable.

1 81

2 36

3 97

4 140

Find the cube root of each number. Round each answer to the nearest tenth where applicable.

5 216

6 343

7 682

8 $\dfrac{27}{512}$

Solve each equation. Round each answer to the nearest tenth where applicable.

9 $h^2 = 50.41$

10 $d^2 = \dfrac{49}{81}$

11 $s^3 = 2,744$

12 $s^3 = \dfrac{27}{343}$

Solve. Round decimal answers to the nearest tenth.

13 8 small metal cubes are melted and recast into a big metal cube. The volume of each small cube is 216 cubic centimeters. What is the side length of the big cube?

14 Alejandro placed 25 cookies on a square tray. Each cookie occupies a square base area of 16 square centimeters. What is the length of the tray?

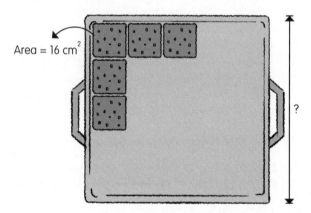

Area = 16 cm^2

?

Mathematical Habit 3 Construct viable arguments

Ryan says that the value of 10^{100} is the same as the value of 100^{10}. Ava says the values are different. Who is correct? Explain.

Ryan's work:
10^{100}
$= 10 \cdot 10^2$
$= 10^{1+2}$
$= 10^3$
$= 1,000$

100^{10}
$= 100 \cdot 10^1$
$= 10^{2+1}$
$= 10^3$
$= 1,000$

So, $10^{100} = 100^{10}$.

Ava's work:
10^{100}

100^{10}
$= (10^2)^{10}$
$= 10^{2 \cdot 10}$
$= 10^{20}$

So, $10^{100} \neq 10^{20}$.

Mathematical Habit 8 **Look for patterns**

The formula $T_n = ar^{n-1}$ can be used to find the nth term of a sequence of numbers, where a is the first term in the sequence and r is the common ratio.

For example, in the sequence 10, 40, 160, 640, …,

$a = 10$, and $r = \dfrac{40}{10} = \dfrac{160}{40} = \dfrac{640}{160} = 4$.

So, $T_n = 10 \cdot 4^{n-1}$

Here is another sequence.

$\dfrac{1}{2}$, 1, 2, 4, 8, 16, …

Use the formula to find the product of the 10th and 13th terms, and when the 10th term is divided by the 13th term. Express your answers in exponential notation.

Chapter 3

Extra Practice and Homework
Scientific Notation

Activity 1   Understanding Scientific Notation

Determine whether each number is written correctly in scientific notation.
If it is incorrectly written, state the reason.

① $21.5 \cdot 10^{-4}$

② $9 \cdot 10^{15}$

③ $7.25 \cdot 10^{23}$

④ $0.8 \cdot 10^{7}$

Write each number in scientific notation.

⑤ 6,238

⑥ 3,700,000,000

⑦ 0.00000000000083

⑧ 0.0028

Write each number in standard form.

⑨ $6.05 \cdot 10^{1}$

⑩ $8.4 \cdot 10^{5}$

11 $3.82 \cdot 10^{-4}$

12 $9.8 \cdot 10^{-7}$

Identify the greater number in each pair of numbers. Justify each reasoning.

13 $9.9 \cdot 10^{10}$ and $9.6 \cdot 10^{11}$

14 $5.8 \cdot 10^{5}$ and $8.5 \cdot 10^{3}$

15 $4.8 \cdot 10^{-7}$ and $8.8 \cdot 10^{-7}$

16 $1.25 \cdot 10^{-3}$ and $1.28 \cdot 10^{-5}$

Solve.

17 Diego came across the following fun facts about the human body while searching the internet. Fill in the table by writing each figure in scientific notation.

Fun Facts	Figures in Standard Form	Figures in Scientific Notation
Number of cells in a human body	12,000,000,000,000	
Diameter of a red blood cell (m)	0.0000084	
Average number of times the human eye blinks in a year	10,200,000	
Number of strands of hair on human scalp	100,000	
Width of a strand of human hair (cm)	0.00108	
Average number of times a human heart beats in its lifetime	3,000 million	

18 Airborne particles are solids suspended in the air. The table shows the sizes of some airborne particles.

Airborne Particles	Particle Diameter (m) in Standard Form	Particle Diameter in Scientific Notation (m)
Sawdust	0.000085	
Talcum powder dust	0.00000024	
Carbon dust	0.0000007	
Cement dust	0.000018	

a Fill in the table by writing each particle diameter in scientific notation.

b The human eye can see particles to approximately $4 \cdot 10^{-5}$ meter. Which airborne particles listed in the table are visible to humans?

19 The table shows the speeds of two types of energy in air.

Energy	Speed (m/s)	Speed in Scientific Notation (m/s)
Light	300 million	
Sound	330	

a Fill in the table by writing the speed of each type of energy in scientific notation.

b There was a thunderstorm. Riley says she saw a flash of lightning before she heard the sound of thunder. Is she correct? Explain.

20 At a science fair, Katelyn came across the following data:

- The average human eye blink takes $3.5 \cdot 10^5$ microseconds.
- A camera flash illuminates for 1,000 microseconds.
- The shutter speed of a standard camera is $4 \cdot 10^3$ microseconds.

Note: A microsecond is a unit of time that is equal to one-millionth (10^{-6}) of a second. Its symbol is μs.

a Which action listed takes the least amount of time, in microseconds, to complete? Write your answer in scientific notation.

b Which action listed takes the greatest amount of time, in microseconds, to complete? Write the time taken, in seconds, in scientific notation.

Chapter 3

Extra Practice and Homework
Scientific Notation

Activity 2   Adding and Subtracting in Scientific Notation

Evaluate each expression. Write each answer in scientific notation.

1 $7.8 \cdot 10^5 + 3.9 \cdot 10^5$

2 $11.4 \cdot 10^{-3} - 9.8 \cdot 10^{-3}$

3 $5.6 \cdot 10^{-2} + 8.6 \cdot 10^{-1}$

4 $6.5 \cdot 10^7 - 2.8 \cdot 10^6$

Make sure the numbers have the same power of 10 before adding or subtracting.

Solve.

5 The driving distance between Phoenix and Los Angeles is 599 kilometers.
The driving distance between Phoenix and Chicago is approximately $2.3 \cdot 10^3$ kilometers.

a Which city is nearer to Phoenix, Los Angeles, or Chicago?

b Mr. Martin traveled from Phoenix to Los Angeles and Ms. Norton traveled from Phoenix to Chicago. What is the difference beween the distances traveled? Write your answer in scientific notation.

6 The diagram shows a small ant and a large ant.

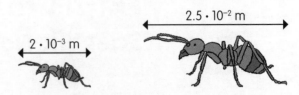

The length of the small ant is $2 \cdot 10^{-3}$ meter and the length of the large ant is $2.5 \cdot 10^{-2}$ meter.

a Find the difference in length, in millimeters, between the two ants. Write your answer in scientific notation.

b There is a trail of 2 small ants and 1 large ant in a straight line. Find the total length, in millimeters, of the trail. Write your answer in scientific notation.

7 An atom of hydrogen has a mass of 1.6×10^{-24} gram. An atom of oxygen has a mass of 2.6×10^{-23} gram. A molecule of water contains 1 atom of oxygen and 2 atoms of hydrogen.

a Find the difference in mass between an atom of hydrogen and an atom of oxygen. Write your answer in scientific notation.

b Find the mass of 1 molecule of water. Write your answer in scientific notation.

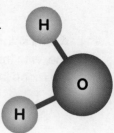

8 The Sun is 150 million kilometers from the Earth. The Moon is 400 thousand kilometers from the Earth.

  a A total lunar eclipse happens when the positions of the Sun, Earth, and Moon are in a straight line, with the Earth between the Sun and the Moon. Find the distance between the Sun and the Moon in scientific notation.

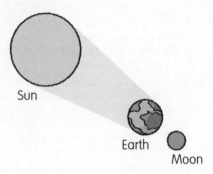

  b A total solar eclipse happens when the positions of the Sun, Earth, and Moon are in a straight line, with the Moon between the Sun and the Earth. Find the distance between the Sun and the Moon in scientific notation.

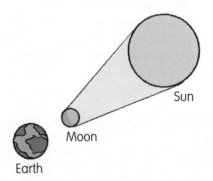

Chapter 3
Extra Practice and Homework
Scientific Notation

Activity 3 Multiplying and Dividing in Scientific Notation

Evaluate each expression. Write each answer in scientific notation and round the coefficient to the nearest tenth where applicable.

1 $8.5 \cdot 10^{-2} \cdot 9.52 \cdot 10^{7}$

2 $3.8 \cdot 10^{3} \div (4.86 \cdot 10^{-2})$

3 $6.2 \cdot 10^{5} \cdot 4.7 \cdot 10^{-8}$

4 $6.8 \cdot 10^{10} \div (2.3 \cdot 10^{-4})$

 Solve.

5 The approximate radius of Virus K is between $3 \cdot 10^{-8}$ meter and $1.1 \cdot 10^{-7}$ meter.

a Express the range of this diameter in prefix form using nanometers.

b A virus of diameter 48 nanometers has just been detected in a small community. Use the diameter to predict if this newly detected virus is a Virus K.

6 A certain type of bacteria can move at a speed of 220 micrometers per second.

a What is the distance, in meters, moved by the bacteria after 12 hours? Write your answer in scientific notation.

b Another type of bacteria moves $8 \cdot 10^{-7}$ meter per second. How far does this bacteria move in $5.45 \cdot 10^9$ seconds? Write your answer, in micrometers, using scientific notation.

7 The diagram shows a cube with sides of length 8 meters. A small cube with sides of length 3 meters has been cut out of the large cube.

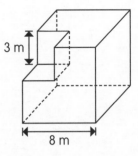

a Find the volume, in cubic centimeters, of the large cube before the small cube is cut out. Write your answer in scientific notation.

b Find the volume, in cubic centimeters, of the solid after the small cube is removed. Write your answer in scientific notation.

8 The distance between Town A and Town B is 10 megameters while that between Town A and Town C is 100 kilometers. Is Town B or Town C nearer to Town A? Explain.

9 The length and width of a rectangular pool are 25 meters and 9 meters respectively.
It contains water to a depth of 1.2 meters.

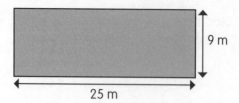

9 m

25 m

a Express the measurements in centimeters using the scientific notation.

b Find the volume of water in the pool in liters using the scientific notation.
Note: $1 \text{ cm}^3 = 1 \text{ mL}$ and $1 \text{ L} = 10^3 \text{ mL}$

c A pump drains out water at a rate of 48 liters per second. How long, to the nearest minute,
does it take to empty the pool?

Mathematical Habit 3 Construct viable arguments

Anna evaluated the expression as shown.

$(2.6 \cdot 10^3) \cdot (4.8 \cdot 10^4) \div (2.4 \cdot 10^5)$

$= (2.6 \cdot 4.8 \div 2.4) \cdot 10^3 \cdot 10^4 \cdot 10^5$

$= 5.2 \cdot 10^{3+4+5}$

$= 5.2 \cdot 10^{12}$

Was Anna's solution correct? Explain.

1 **Mathematical Habit 1** Persevere in solving problems

Given that $p = 2 \cdot 10^{-3}$ and $q = 3 \cdot 10^{-2}$, find the value of each expression.

a $\quad 3q - 4p$

b $\quad \dfrac{2q}{p}$

2 **Mathematical Habit 8** Look for patterns

Without using a calculator, evaluate $\sqrt{\dfrac{3 \cdot 10^9 \cdot 1.8 \cdot 10^{-4}}{2 \cdot 10^{-2} \cdot 4.8 \cdot 10^{11}}}$, giving your answer in scientific notation.

Chapter 4
Extra Practice and Homework
Linear Equations and Inequalities

Activity 1   Solving Linear Equations with One Variable

Solve each linear equation.

1 $5x - 4 = 2x + 5$

2 $3x + 0.5(10x - 6) = 21$

3 $4(x + 2) - 2(x - 4) = 32$

4 $8 - 3(x + 2) = 2(4 - 3x) - 4.5$

5 $\dfrac{2(2x + 1)}{5} - \dfrac{x + 2}{3} = \dfrac{1}{5}$

6 $\dfrac{x + 3}{2} - \dfrac{11 - x}{5} = 1 + \dfrac{3x - 1}{20}$

Write each repeating decimal as a fraction.

7 $0.\overline{4}$

8 $0.0\overline{3}$

9 $0.2\overline{5}$

10 $0.3\overline{18}$

Solve each problem algebraically.

11 Mr. Williams bought $3\frac{1}{2}$ pounds of ground meat and $2\frac{1}{2}$ pounds of white fish. The white fish is $4.60 per pound cheaper than the ground meat. He paid a total of $51.50. What is the price per pound he paid for the ground meat, and the price per pound for the white fish?

Let the cost price per pound for the ground meat be x dollars.

12 Gavin is x years old now. Two years ago, his grandfather was 3 times older than Gavin at that time.

a The age difference between Gavin and his grandfather is 48 years. Write a linear equation to represent this age difference.

b Find Gavin's grandfather's age now.

13 There are 40 students in a class. The teacher gave each female student 5 counters and each male student 3 counters. After the distribution of the counters, the teacher realized that the female students had 128 more counters than the male students. Write and solve a linear equation to find the number of female students in the class.

14 Hunter has 3 bamboo poles of different lengths. The total combined length of the 3 poles when placed end-to-end is $47\frac{1}{2}$ inches long. Pole B is $1\frac{3}{4}$ times as long as Pole A, and Pole C is $2\frac{1}{2}$ inches longer than Pole A.

a Write a linear equation for the total combined length of the 3 poles.

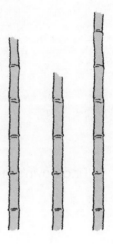

b Find the length of Pole C.

Extra Practice and Homework
Linear Equations and Inequalities

Chapter 4

Activity 2   Identifying the Number of Solutions to a Linear Equation

Determine whether each equation is a consistent equation, an inconsistent equation, or an identity.

1 $\frac{4}{5}x + 18 = -2(3 + 2x)$

2 $7 + 2(x - 6) = -3 + 2(x - 1)$

3 $2\left(4 - \frac{1}{3}x\right) = x + 3(x - 2)$

4 $\frac{2}{5}(1 - 5x) = -\frac{1}{2}(4x + 3)$

5 $5(5 - 2x) - 6(2 - x) = 7(1 - x)$

6 $0.5(3x + 5) - 0.1(12x - 5) = 3(1 + 0.1x)$

7 $4(2 - x) + 2(1 - 5x) = 5(2 - 3x) + x$

8 $3\left(\frac{2}{9}x - 1\right) = 1 - \frac{2}{3}(x + 1) + \frac{4}{3}x$

9 $2(x + 5) - 2 = 1.5(10 - x)$

10 $2(x - 3) + \frac{1}{2}(7 + 2x) = \frac{1}{2} + 3(x - 1)$

11 $8.2(x + 5) = 15 - 0.8(x - 10)$

12 $9(x - 4) - 0.6(x + 6) = 7 + 0.7(1 + 12x)$

Solve.

13 The diagram shows an isosceles triangle *ABC*. The length of *AB* is $(3x - 5)$ inches and the length of *AC* is $(45 - 2x)$ inches.

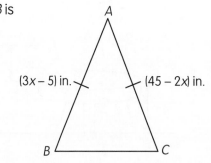

  a Form an equation in *x*.

  b Determine whether the equation in **a** is consistent. If so, find the length of *AB*.

14 The diagram shows a rhombus *WXYZ*. The length of *WX* is $\left(\dfrac{x+2}{2} + 1\right)$ centimeters and

the length of *YZ* is $\left(\dfrac{x+4}{2}\right)$ centimeters.

  a Form an equation in *x*.

  b Can you solve for the length of *WX*? Explain.

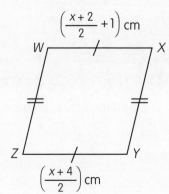

15 The diagram shows 3 three-legged stools of different heights.

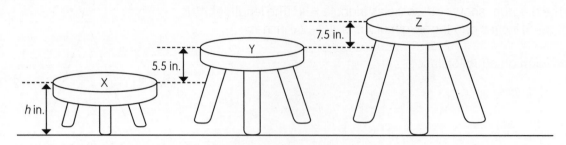

a Write algebraic expressions for the heights of Stool Y and Stool Z.

b Jack says that twice the height of Stool Z is equal to the sum of the height of Stool X and Stool Y. Do you think he is correct? Explain.

16 In figure $ABCD$, the length of AB is $6\left(3 - \frac{1}{4}x\right)$ centimeters and the length of AD is $\left(\frac{3}{4}x + 5 - 2\frac{1}{4}x\right)$ centimeters. With these dimensions, can you conclude that the figure is a square? Explain.

$$A \quad \overset{6\left(3 - \frac{1}{4}x\right)\text{cm}}{\rule{3cm}{0.4pt}} \quad B$$

$\left(\frac{3}{4}x + 5 - 2\frac{1}{4}x\right)$ cm   ?

D   C

Chapter 4

Extra Practice and Homework
Linear Equations and Inequalities

Activity 3   Understanding Linear Equations with Two Variables

Write a linear equation for the relationship between the given quantities.

1 kilometers, k, and meters, m

2 pounds, p, and ounces, u

3 days, d, and hours, h

4 megabytes, m, and bytes, b

Find the value of y when $x = -3$.

5 $4 - 2x = 8 + y$

6 $y = \dfrac{5}{4}(x + 7)$

7 $3(y - 5) = 5x + 3$

8 $7(x - 3) = 6y$

Find the value of x when $y = 5$.

9 $3(x - 3) = 2y$

10 $\dfrac{5x - 3}{2} = 2(y + 3)$

11 $3x + 2y = 0.2(2y + 1)$

12 $7y - 4x = 51$

Create a table of x- and y-values for each equation. Use integer values of x from 2 to 4.

13 $y = \dfrac{1}{3}(9x - 18)$

14 $3x - 4 = \dfrac{1}{5}(y - 5)$

15 $-7y = 4x - 3$

16 $\frac{1}{4}(6x + 1) = \frac{1}{2}(y + 2)$

Fill in the table of values for each equation.

17 $y = 4(2x + 1)$

x	1	2	3
y			

18 $x + \frac{y}{3} = 2$

x			3
y	9	3	

Remember to substitute the correct value for x to find y and for y to find x.

19 $4(y - 3x) = \dfrac{4}{5}$

x		1	2
y	$\dfrac{1}{5}$		

20 $3x = 5(y - 7)$

x			
y	−5	10	25

Solve.

21 Howard has $40 in his bank account. He plans to add $7.50 a week when he starts his summer vacation job.

    a Write a linear equation for the amount in his bank account, *A* dollars, in terms of the amount of time he worked, *t* weeks.

    b Create a table of *t* and *A* values for the linear equation. Use *t* = 4, 6, and 8.

    c Find the number of weeks that Howard will have to save to buy a $175 season pass to a theme park.

(22) A tank initially contains 50 liters of water. A faucet adds water to the tank at a rate of 2 liters per minute.

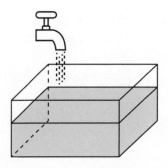

a Write a linear equation for the amount of water in the tank, *W* liters, in terms of *t* minutes.

b Use the equation in **a** to complete the table of values below.

Time (*t* minutes)	20			80
Amount of Water in Tank (*W* liters)		130	170	210

c How much water is in the tank after 5 hours?

d The tank can hold 1,000 liters of water when filled completely. How long will it take to completely fill the tank? Write your answer in hours and minutes.

Ms. White sells sunscreen at a beach kiosk station. Each week, she receives, in salary, $90 plus $0.25 for each tube of sunscreen that she sells.

a Write a linear equation for her weekly salary, *M*, in terms of the number of tubes of sunscreen sold, *n*. Then, use the equation to create a table of values for *M* and *n* using the linear formula. Use *n* = 64, 76, 88, and 100.

b What was Ms. White's salary for the week if she sold 360 tubes of sunscreen last week?

c Ms. White's salary for a particular week was $130. How many tubes of sunscreen did she sell that week?

Extra Practice and Homework
Linear Equations and Inequalities

Chapter 4

Activity 4   Solving for a Variable in a Two-Variable Linear Equation

Express y in terms of x. Find the value of y when x = –2.

1 $4 - 2y = 5x - 3$

2 $2(x + 1) = 7 - y$

3 $4(3x - y) = 10$

4 $7 - 3x = 2y - 0.6x$

5 $\frac{3}{5}x - \frac{1}{3}y = 4$

6 $1.2y + 3 = 0.36x$

Express x in terms of y. Find the value of x when $y = 4$.

7 $4y + x = 5(2x - y)$

8 $-2(x + 3y) = x + 6y$

9 $2.5(x - 2y) = 10$

10 $6y + 9 = \frac{2}{3}x$

11 $\frac{2(3x - 2)}{y} = 12$

12 $\frac{1}{4}(3 - 2x) = \frac{3y}{8}$

Solve.

13 The diagram shows a quadrant of a circle with a radius of r centimeters.

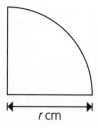

r cm

  a Express the perimeter of the quadrant, P centimeters, in terms of the radius, r centimeters.

  b Express r in terms of P.

  c Find the radius given that the perimeter is 50 centimeters. Use $\frac{22}{7}$ as an approximation for π.

14 A restaurant has x number of tables that can seat four people and 5 tables that can seat two people. The restaurant can seat a total of N people.

  a Write a linear equation for the total number of people, N, in terms of x.

  b Express x in terms of N.

  c Find the value of x when $N = 150$.

15 Mr. Flores bought a sapling from a tree nursery and observed a linear growth of the sapling over a period of 6 months. He found that the height of the sapling, H centimeters, and the time, t months, is related by the linear equation $H = 2(4 + 3t)$.

a Write an equation for t in terms of H.

b Complete the table below.

Height (H centimeters)		20	26	
Time (t months)	1			4

c Find the value of H when $t = 6$.

d How many months did the sapling take to reach a height of 29 centimeters?

Chapter 4

Extra Practice and Homework
Linear Equations and Inequalities

Activity 5   Solving Linear Inequalities with One Variable

Solve each inequality and graph the solution set on a number line.

1 $4x - 2 > 8 + 2x$

2 $x - 8 < 3x + 4$

3 $2.3x - 3 \geq 1.8x + 2$

4 $12.3 - 0.4x > 0.1x + 6.1$

5 $\dfrac{2}{3}x + \dfrac{1}{4} \geq \dfrac{1}{6}x + \dfrac{7}{8}$

6 $\dfrac{4}{9}x - \dfrac{3}{4} < \dfrac{1}{3}x - \dfrac{5}{8}$

Solve.

7 Marissa's scores for 4 Math tests are 71, 81, 77, and 69. What is the least score she must achieve in the next test to have an average score of at least 75?

8 Boston School's management team plans to buy some desks and chairs for a new student corner. They need to buy 40 more chairs than desks. The chairs cost $32 each and the desks cost $48 each. Given that the budget is $5,000, what is the maximum number of chairs and desks they can buy?

Name: _____ Date: _____

Mathematical Habit 4 Use mathematical models

The total edge length of a rectangular box is 120 centimeters. The length of the box is 1 centimeter longer than the width of the box. The height of the box is 1 centimeter shorter than the width of the box. Destiny wants to find the dimensions of the box. Show how to form an equation to find the dimensions of the box.

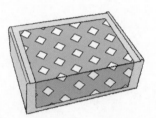

MATH JOURNAL

1 **Mathematical Habit 1** Persevere in solving problems

Solve the following equation.

$$\frac{p+3}{p-3} = \frac{3}{2} + 1$$

2 **Mathematical Habit 4** Use mathematical models

Mr. Cook roasted some almonds for his students. If he gives each student 7 almonds, he will have 26 almonds left. If he gives each student 10 almonds, he will be short of 25 almonds. Using a linear equation, calculate the number of students in Mr. Cook's class. Then, find the number of almonds that he roasted.

Name: _____ Date: _____

Chapter 5

Extra Practice and Homework
Lines and Linear Equations

Activity 1   Finding and Interpreting Slopes of Lines

Find the slope of each line.

1

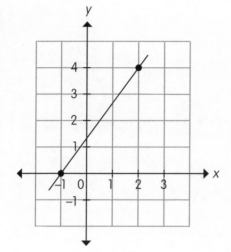

2

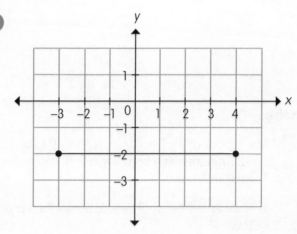

3

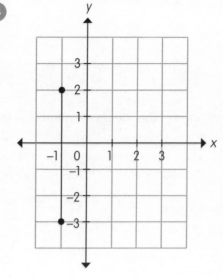

4

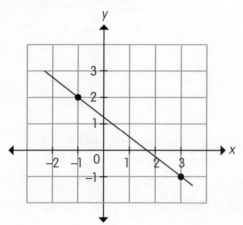

Find the slope of the line passing through each pair of points.

5 $P(4, 5)$ and $Q(0, -3)$

6 $W(9, -2)$ and $X(9, 8)$

7 $R(-8, 2)$ and $S(-3, -3)$

8 $Y(7, 4)$ and $Z(3, 4)$

Solve.

9 Ms. Moore drove her car from Town P to Town Q. She drove at a constant speed. She was 85 kilometers away from Town P in 1 hour. She reached Town Q, that is 340 kilometers away from Town P, in 4 hours.

a Translate the verbal descriptions into a pair of points in the form (time taken, distance from Town P).

b Find the slope of the line passing through the pair of points in **a**.

10 The vertices of a triangle are $A(-3, -2)$, $B(-2, 5)$ and $C(4, -2)$. Find the slopes of the sides of the triangle.

To find the slope of *AB*, use the coordinates of *A* and of *B*.

11 The graph on the left shows the relationship between the distance traveled, *d* kilometers, by Car A over time, *t* hours. The graph on the right shows the relationship between the distance traveled, *d* kilometers, by Car B over time, *t* hours.

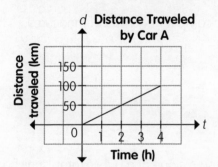

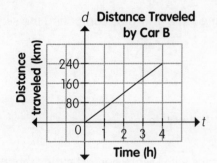

a Find the slopes of the line graphs for Car A and for Car B.

b Which graph is steeper?

12 An architect is designing an accessibility ramp to be used at the entrance of a convention center.

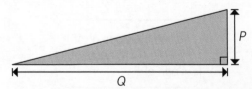

The table shows the different measures of P and Q, in feet, that the architect is considering.

Height (P feet)	Length (Q feet)	Slope of Ramp
3	60	
5	50	
3	36	
2	30	

a Complete the table above by computing the slope of the ramp for each set of measures.

b The Americans with Disabilities Act states that the maximum slope of a public ramp shall be 1 : 12. Which of the ramps in a has a slope of 1 : 12?

c Which ramp is the steepest?

Extra Practice and Homework
Lines and Linear Equations

Activity 2 Understanding Slope-Intercept Form

Identify the *y*-intercept. Then, calculate the slope using the points indicated.

1

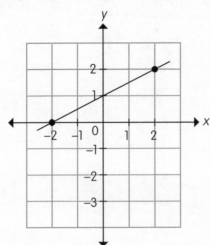

2

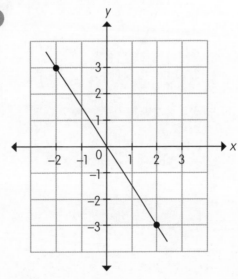

3

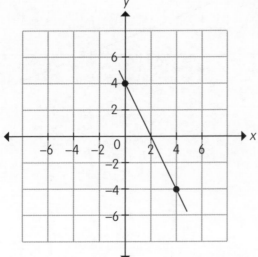

4

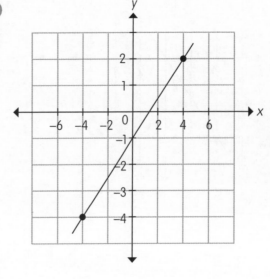

Write an equation in the form $y = mx$ or $y = mx + b$ for each line.

5

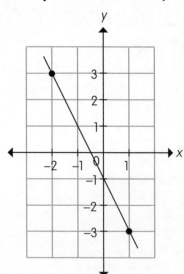

6

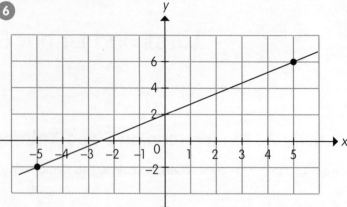

7

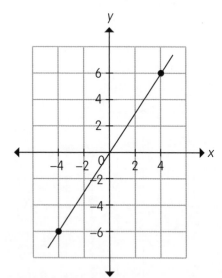

8

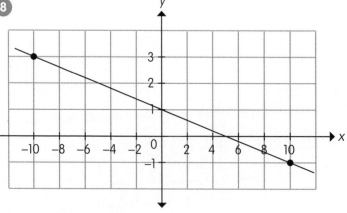

Graph each line using 1 grid square to represent 1 unit using the interval given. Then, write the equation for each line.

9 *x*-axis: −4 to 4
y-axis: −3 to 1
The line passes through the points (−2, −2) and (4, −2).

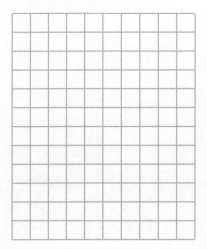

10 *x*-axis: −4 to 4
y-axis: −4 to 5
The line passes through the points (3, 5) and (3, −4).

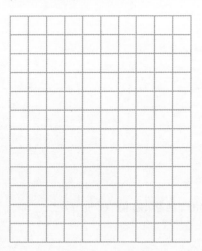

11 *x*-axis: −4 to 4
y-axis: −4 to 5
The line passes through the points (0, −4) and (0, 5).

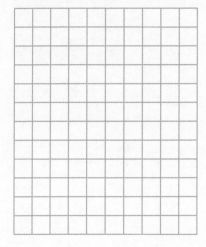

12 *x*-axis: −4 to 4
y-axis: −1 to 1
The line passes through the points (4, 0) and (−3, 0).

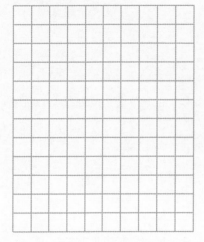

2 Understanding Slope-Intercept Form

Graph the lines using 1 grid square to represent 1 unit on both axes.

13 The line passes through the points $A(0, -4)$ and $B(-3, -2)$, and another line passes through $C(8, 0)$ and $D(0, -2)$.

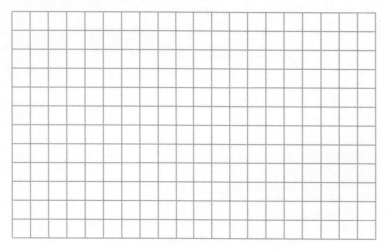

a Find the equation of line AB.

b Find the equation of line CD.

Chapter 5 Extra Practice and Homework
Lines and Linear Equations

Activity 3   Writing Linear Equations

Find the slope and the y-intercept of each line.

1 $y = 4x - 7$

2 $y = -x + 3$

3 $4x - 3y = 9$

4 $-5x + 2y = 6$

Use the given slope and the y-intercept of each line to write an equation in slope-intercept form.

5 Slope, $m = \dfrac{2}{3}$

  y-intercept, $b = 1$

6 Slope, $m = -5$

  y-intercept, $b = 2$

Solve.

7 A line has the equation $4x - 3y + 9 = 0$. Write the equation of a line parallel to this line that has a y-intercept of -1.

8 A line has the equation $2y = -3x + 1$. Write the equation of a line parallel to this line that has a y-intercept of -2.

9 A line has slope $-\dfrac{3}{4}$ and passes through the point (8, 3). Write the equation of the line.

10 Write the equation of the line that passes through the point (3, −5) and is parallel to $4x = 1 + 2y$.

11 Write the equation of the line that passes through the point (7, 0) and is parallel to $7y = 6x - 14$.

12 Write the equation of the line that passes through the pair of points (1, −6) and (−4, 9).

13 Write the equation of the line that passes through the pair of points (3, −10) and (0, 11).

Chapter 5

Extra Practice and Homework
Lines and Linear Equations

Activity 4   Sketching Graphs of Linear Equations

Graph each linear equation. Use 1 grid square to represent 1 unit on both axes for the interval from −6 to 6.

1 $y = \frac{2}{3}x + 2$

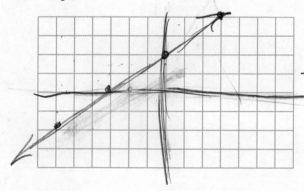

$$\frac{Rise\ 2}{Run\ 3} \left(\frac{2}{3} \right)$$

Remember to construct a table of values to graph the linear equation.

2 $y = \frac{3}{4}x - 5$

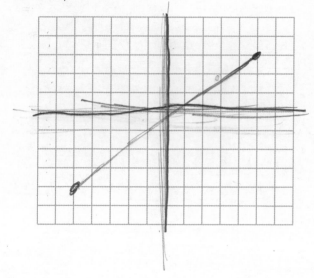

3 $y = \frac{3}{5}x + 3$

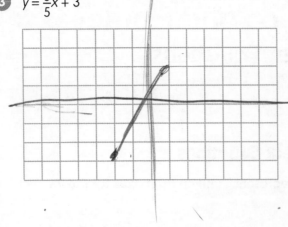

4 $y = 5 - 2x$

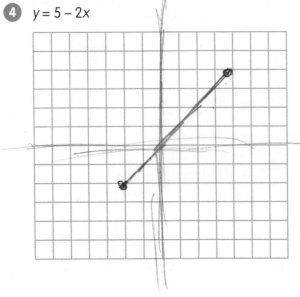

5 $y = 2 - \dfrac{1}{6}x$

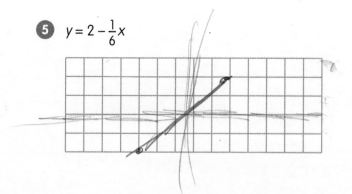

6 $y = \dfrac{4}{3}x - 4$

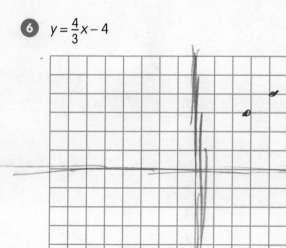

7 $y = 2x + 3$

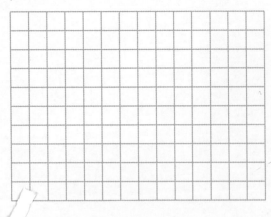

8 $y = -2 - x$

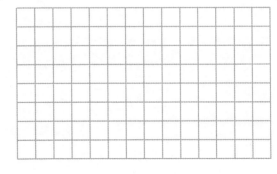

Graph each line.

9 A line with slope 2 that passes through the point (2, 5)

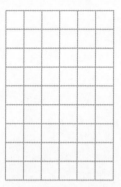

10 A line with slope $-\dfrac{4}{5}$ that passes through the point (−5, 6)

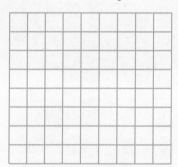

11 A line with slope −1 that passes through the point (3, 2)

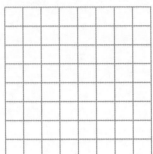

12 A line with slope $\frac{3}{2}$ that passes through the point (−2, −4)

Chapter

Extra Practice and Homework
Lines and Linear Equations

Activity 5   Real-World Problems: Linear Equations

Solve.

1 To rent a bike, Wyatt pays a flat rate plus an hourly rental fee. The graph shows the cost, C dollars, based on the number of hours used, t.

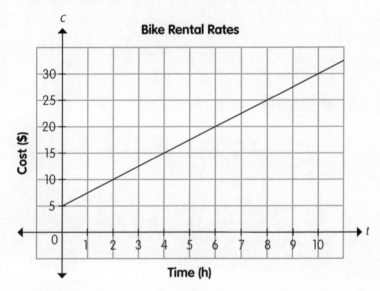

a Find the vertical intercept of the graph and explain what information it gives about the situation.

b Find the slope of the graph and explain what information it gives about the situation.

c Find the amount Wyatt pays to rent a bike for 6 hours.

2 The growth of two plant saplings, A and B, was observed for a period of 6 months. The graph shows the linear growth of the saplings, in centimeters.

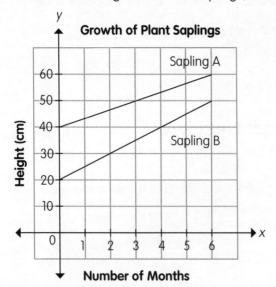

a Find the initial heights of Sapling A and Sapling B.

b Which sapling showed a greater amount of growth during the 6 month time period? Explain.

3 The graph shows the cost, C, of renting a concert hall for t hours.

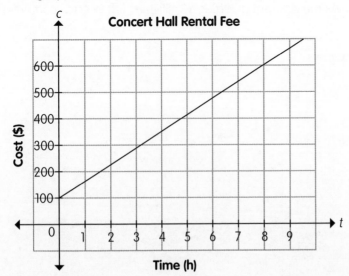

Concert Hall Rental Fee

a Find the vertical intercept of the graph and explain what information it gives about the situation.

b Find the slope of the graph and explain what information it gives about the situation.

4 Two containers, P and Q, are filled with different amounts of water. Each container has a tap draining water from it. The graph shows the amount of water, V milliliters, left in each container after x minutes.

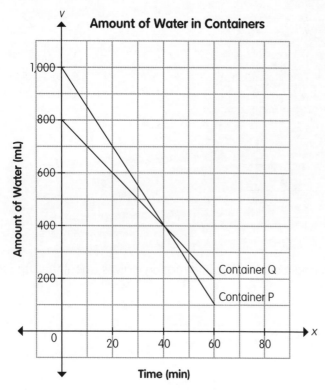

a Find the initial amount of water in each container.

b Which container's tap drains water faster? Explain.

5 A candle is 9 inches long. Kyle lights the candle and records the length of the candle, *y* inches, for *x* hours.

Number of Hours Candle Burns (x hours)	0	1	2	3	4
Height of Candle (y inches)	9	7	5	3	1

a Graph the relationship between candle height and time. Use 2 grid squares to represent 1 unit on the horizontal axis for the *x*-interval 0 to 4 and 1 grid square for 1 unit on the vertical axis for the *y*-interval 0 to 9.

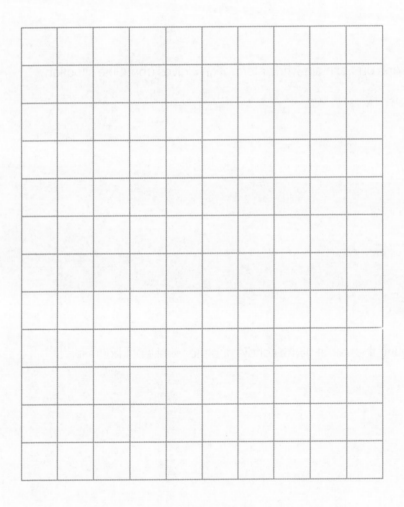

b Find the vertical intercept of the graph and explain what information it gives about the situation.

c Find the slope of the graph and explain what information it gives about the situation.

d Write the equation relating the height of the candle and the number of hours it is lit.

Name: _____ Date: _____

Mathematical Habit **6** **Use precise mathematical language**

The graph shows two lines, $y = 3x + 1$ and $y = x - 2$.

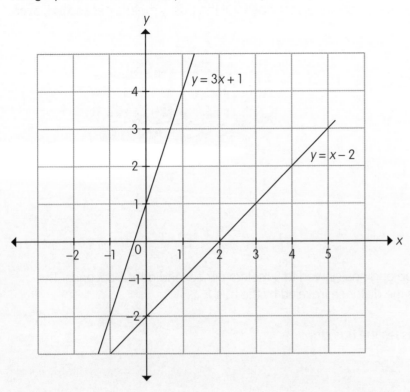

With the help of the two given lines, sketch the graph of $y = 2x - 1$ on the grid above. Explain how you draw the graph.

Mathematical Habit **1** **Persevere in solving problems**

A bus driver is deciding if he should stop at a particular bus stop. When he drives towards the bus stop, he begins to reduce his speed. The graph shows the speed of the bus, y meters per second, over t seconds.

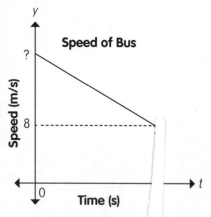

The bus is 50 meters behind the stop and has slowed to 8 meters per second after 5 seconds. The area under the speed-time graph is the distance traveled by the bus.

a Find the speed of the bus as it passes the bus stop.

b Find the rate at which the bus slowed down, assuming it to be constant.

c Write the equation to represent the speed of the bus, y meters per second, after t seconds.

Chapter 6

Extra Practice and Homework
Systems of Linear Equations

Handwritten work in margins:
$2(2)-3y=3$
$4-3y=3$
-4 -4
$-3y=\dfrac{-1}{-3}$
$y=-\dfrac{1}{3}$
$2(3)-3y=3$
-6 -6

Activity 1   Introduction to Systems of Linear Equations

Solve each system of linear equations by making tables of values. *x* is a positive integer less than 6.

1 $x + 3y = 6$
$2x - 3y = 3$

Handwritten work:
$2(1)-3y=3$
$2-3y=3$
-2
$3y=1$
$y=-\dfrac{1}{3}$

$1+3y=6$
-1 -1
$3y=5$
$\dfrac{3y}{3}=\dfrac{5}{3}$
$y=\dfrac{5}{3}$

x	1	2	3	4	5
y	$\frac{5}{3}$	$\frac{4}{3}$	1	$\frac{2}{3}$	$\frac{1}{3}$

x		2	3	4	5
y	$-\frac{1}{2}$				

$2+3y=6$
-2
$\dfrac{3y}{3}=\dfrac{5}{3}$

$\dfrac{3y}{3}=\dfrac{4}{3}$
$y=\dfrac{4}{3}$

2 $2x - y = 1$
$2x + 3y = 13$

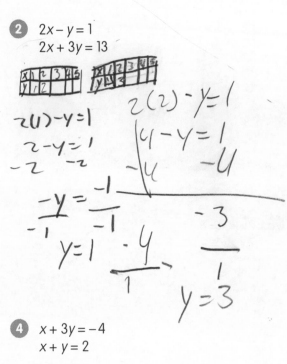

Handwritten work:
$2(1)-y=1$
$2-y=1$
-2 -2
$\dfrac{-y}{-1}=\dfrac{-1}{-1}$
$y=1$

$2(2)-y=1$
$4-y=1$
-4 -4
$\dfrac{-3}{1}$
$y=3$

x	2	3	4	5
y	1			

3 $3x - y = 2$
$2x = y$

Empty table with x and y rows

4 $x + 3y = -4$
$x + y = 2$

5 $2x + y = 10$
$2x - y = 6$

6 $x - y = -2$
$3x + y = 6$

7 $2y - x = 8$
$2x - y = -1$

8 $3x + 4y = 15$
$3x = y$

Solve by making tables of values. The values of *x* and *y* are positive integers.

9 Hannah takes *x* minutes to fold a paper airplane and *y* minutes to fold a paper star. On a particular day, she folded 5 paper airplanes and 4 paper stars in 64 minutes. The following day, she folded 3 paper airplanes and 8 paper stars in 72 minutes. The related system of linear equations is:

$5x + 4y = 64$
$3x + 8y = 72$

Solve the system of linear equations. Then, find the time taken to fold a paper airplane and a paper star.

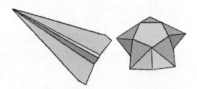

Since time is positive, the values of *x* and *y* are positive.

1 Introduction to Systems of Linear Equations

10 Mr. Perez is training for a biathlon event. On one training day, he walked for 2 hours and cycled for an hour, covering 18 miles in the morning. In the afternoon, he walked for 2 hours and cycled for 3 hours, covering 42 miles. The related system of linear equations where x miles per hour is his walking speed and y miles per hour is his cycling speed, is:

$2x + y = 18$
$2x + 3y = 42$

Solve the system of linear equations by making tables of values. Then, find the difference between Mr. Perez's walking speed and cycling speed.

Extra Practice and Homework
Systems of Linear Equations

Activity 2   Solving Systems of Linear Equations Using Algebraic Methods

Solve each system of linear equations using the elimination method.

1 $3y - x = 2$
    $3y + x = 16$

2 $x - 5y = 13$
    $9y - x = -17$

3 $7q + 2p = 29$
    $2p - q = 5$

4 $2w - 3v = 4$
    $w + 3v = 29$

5 $2a - b = 6$
   $3a + b = 19$

6 $6n - m = 3$
   $3m - 6n = 15$

7 $8x + 6y = 14$
   $6x + 3y = 6$

8 $4p + 5q = -18$
   $3p - 10q = 69$

Solve each system of linear equations using the substitution method.

9 $3a - b = 13$
$b = 2a - 7$

10 $5p + 3q = -7$
$q = -2p + 5$

11 $6c - b = 5$
$b - c = 5$

12 $2y - x = 3$
$y - x = 4$

13 $4h + k = 7$
$h + 2k = 7$

14 $3x + 2y = 36$
$5y - x = 39$

15 $5t + 2s = -3$
$7t - 2s = 15$

16 $5x + 4y = -26$
$5 - x = -6y$

Extra Practice and Homework Course 3A

Solve each system of linear equations using the elimination method or the substitution method. Explain why you choose the method.

17 $3x + 5y = 35$
    $6x - 4y = -28$

18 $7m - 2n = -13$
    $2n - 5m = 11$

19 $9m + 4n = 38$
    $2m = 5n - 21$

20 $5w - 4v = 1$
    $v = 6w + 14$

21 $2h + 9k = 19$
$5h - 5k = 20$

22 $5y + 9 = 3x$
$3x - 2y = 18$

23 $3b + 4c = -6$
$7b + 16c = -34$

24 $7p - q = 18$
$3p + 4q = 21$

Extra Practice and Homework Course 3A

Chapter 6

Extra Practice and Homework
Systems of Linear Equations

Activity 3   Real-World Problems: Systems of Linear Equations

Solve using systems of linear equations.

1. Ms. Parker purchased 26 magazines for her project research at a total cost of $134. The art related magazines cost $4 each, while the science related magazines cost $7 each. Find the number of art related magazines and science related magazines Ms. Parker purchased.

2. A total of 95 theme park tickets were sold for $960. Each adult ticket cost $12 and each child ticket cost $9. Find the number of adult tickets and the number of child tickets sold.

3 The diagram shows an equilateral triangular face of a crystal solid with the given sides. Find the values of x and y.

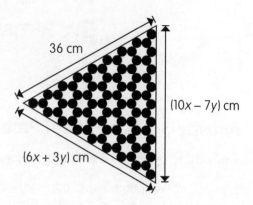

36 cm

$(10x - 7y)$ cm

$(6x + 3y)$ cm

4 Mr. Lopez plans to build a rectangular sandbox for his grandson. He has 26 meters of wood for the perimeter of the sandbox. The length of the sandbox is to be 3 meters longer than the width.

a Write a system of linear equations relating the length, ℓ meters, and width, w meters, of the perimeter of the sandbox.

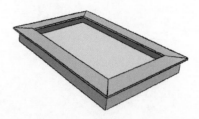

b Find the dimensions of the rectangular sandbox.

5 A vending machine only accepts dimes and quarters. There are 85 coins in the machine with a total value of $16.75. How many of each coin are in the machine?

6 At a fundraising event, a booth was set up to sell handmade cards and photo frames. On the first day, 3 cards and 9 photo frames were sold for a total of $75. The next day, 8 cards and 5 photo frames were sold for a total of $67. Find the selling price of a card and the selling price of a photo frame.

7 Benjamin took a mathematics quiz where he had to solve the following questions.

a The sum of two numbers is 31. Twice the larger number is 7 more than 3 times the smaller number. What are the numbers?

b The sum of a number and twice a second number is 14. When the second number is subtracted from the first number, the difference is 2. Find the two numbers.

8 A tennis club charges an entry fee for the players at the club. The table below shows the money received on a particular Saturday and Sunday.

Day	Number of Senior Players	Number of Junior Players	Entry Fees Charged ($)		Amount of Money Received ($)
			For Seniors	For Juniors	
Saturday	35	20	x	y	310
Sunday	55	45			555

How much is the entry fee for each senior player and each junior player?

9 The table shows the number of words that can be printed on a page for two given font sizes.

Font Size	Number of Words on a Page
Small	1,150
Large	850

Alex needs to print a document with a total of 12,600 words on exactly 12 pages. Find the number of pages in the document that should be printed in small font and the number of pages that should be printed in large font.

Chapter 6

Extra Practice and Homework
Systems of Linear Equations

Activity 4   Solving Systems of Linear Equations by Graphing

Solve each system of linear equations using the graphical method.

1 $x - y = 1$
   $x + 2y = 4$

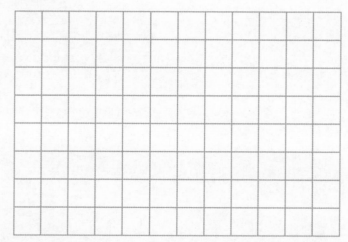

Remember to construct a table of values to graph each system of linear equations.

2 $x - 3y = 5$
   $3x + 2y = 4$

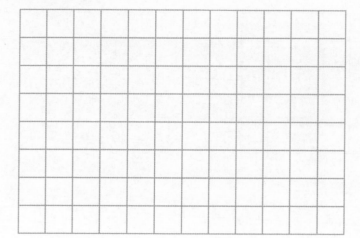

3 $x = 5y$
$y = x - 4$

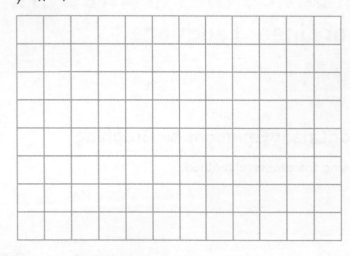

4 $y = 6$
$y = 4x + 4$

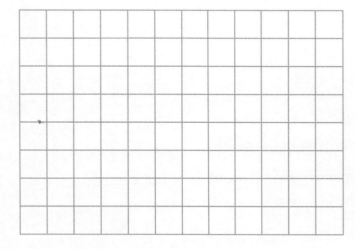

5 $x = 4$
   $y = 3x - 5$

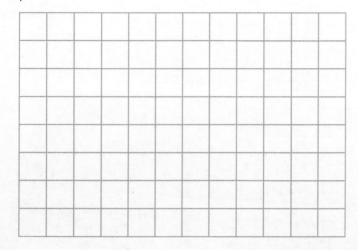

6 $y = 2x + 1$
   $2y = -x + 7$

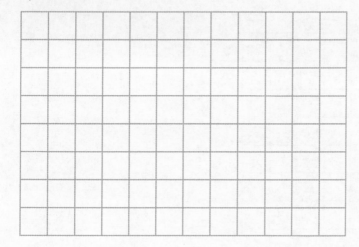

7 $x + 2y = -1$

$4x + y = 3$

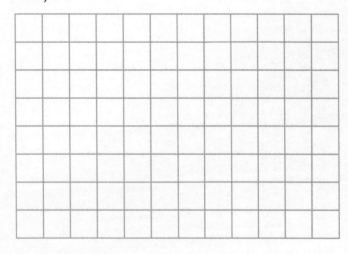

8 $x - 3y = -9$
$5y - x = 15$

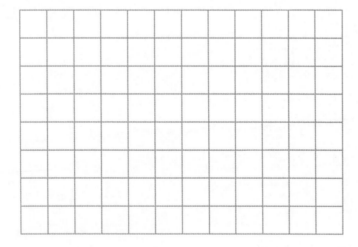

Solve

9 Weights are attached to two different springs. The length of stretch and the amount of weight attached to the springs are described by the linear equations $L = 2w + 1$ and $L = w + 3$, where L inches is the length of the spring stretched and w pounds is the weight attached to each spring.

a Solve the system of linear equations using the graphical method.

b For which weight will the springs stretch the same number of inches?

10 Two vehicles are moving along a straight road in the same direction. Their motions are described by the linear equations $d = 5t + 45$ and $d - 15t = 25$, where t hours is the time and d miles is the distance.

a Solve the system of linear equations using a graphing calculator.

b When will the two vehicles meet?

Chapter

6

Extra Practice and Homework
Systems of Linear Equations

Activity 5   Inconsistent and Dependent Systems of Linear Equations

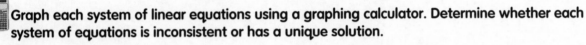

Graph each system of linear equations using a graphing calculator. Determine whether each system of equations is inconsistent or has a unique solution.

1 $2x + y = 11$
$5y = 10x - 5$

2 $2x + 2y = 5$
$10x + 10y = 45$

Determine whether each system of linear equations is inconsistent, dependent, or has a unique solution. Justify each answer. Solve each system of linear equations if it has a unique solution.

3 $8x + 4y = 14$
$2x + y = 28$

4 $12x - 3y = 9$
$4x - y = 3$

5 $-24x + 8y = 4$
$-6x + 2y = 17$

6 $3x + 4y = 22$
$6x - 8y = 28$

7 $4x + 9y = 7$
$16x + 36y = 28$

8 $x + 5y = 17$
$2x + 10y = 11$

9 Mr. Peterson bought some wooden planks of different lengths.

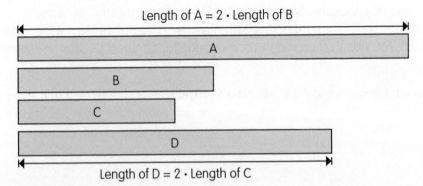

When he places Planks A and D end-to-end, the total length is 16 inches. When he places Planks B and C end-to-end, the total length is 8 inches.

a Write a system of equations to find the length of Plank B and the length of Plank C.

b State with reasons whether the system of equations has a unique solution, is inconsistent, or is independent.

Solve.

10 A lodge claims that it charges all customers the same price for an overnight stay. Similarly, it charges all customers the same price for a meal. Ms. Kim reserved a two-night stay at the lodge, inclusive of 3 meals for $185. Mr. Wilson reserved the same lodge for a four-night stay, inclusive of 6 meals for $350.

a Write a system of linear equations to find the cost of a one-night stay and one meal at the lodge.

b State with reasons whether the system of equations has a unique solution, is inconsistent, or is dependent.

c What does this tell you about the claim made by the lodge?

Mathematical Habit 7 Make use of structure

The total cost of 3 apples and 4 pears is \$3.90. The total cost of 4 apples and 3 pears is \$3.80. Without solving for the cost of each apple or pear, explain how you can find the cost of 1 apple and 1 pear.

1 Mathematical Habit **7** Make use of structure

Dylan gave a riddle to his friend to find the digit code of his cell phone.
It is a 2-digit number.
The sum of the digits of the number is 11.
When the digits are reversed, the value of the number increases by 9.
What is the digit code?

2 Mathematical Habit **8** Look for patterns

The digits 1 through 8 are to be placed in the circles so that the sum of the numbers on each side of the figure is 15. Fill in the appropriate number in each circle.

Note: Each number can only be used once.

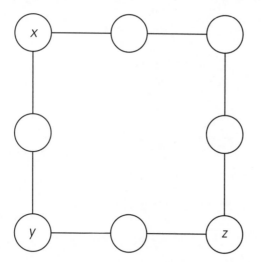

Hint: *x* satisfies the equation $-4(x - 2) = 2 - 2x$,
y satisfies the equation $9 + 2(y - 3) - 3(y - 2) = 1$, and
z satisfies the equation $\frac{z}{3} + \frac{1}{2} = \frac{5}{2}$.

BLANK

BLANK

BLANK

BLANK